# Monster Trucks

## By A.R. Schaefer

**Consultant:**
David Huntoon
Monster Truck Racing Association

CAPSTONE
HIGH-INTEREST
BOOKS

an imprint of Capstone Press
Mankato, Minnesota

Capstone High-Interest Books are published by Capstone Press
151 Good Counsel Drive, P.O. Box 669, Mankato, Minnesota 56002
http://www.capstone-press.com

*Library of Congress Cataloging-in-Publication Data*
Schaefer, Adam.
Monster trucks/by A.R. Schaefer.
    p. cm.—(Wild rides)
    Includes bibliographical references and index.
    ISBN 0-7368-0929-5
    1. Monster trucks—Juvenile literature. [1. Monster trucks. 2. Trucks.]
I. Title. II. Series.
TL230.15 .S32 2002
796.7—dc21                                                                           2001001866

Summary: Describes monster trucks' history, equipment, and competitions.

**Editorial Credits**
Matt Doeden, editor; Karen Risch, product planning editor; Kia Bielke,
    cover and interior designer; Katy Kudela, photo researcher


**Photo Credits**
Action Images/Dave & Bev Huntoon, cover, 4, 6, 7, 8, 10, 13, 14, 16, 19,
20–21, 22, 24, 25, 27, 28

2  3  4  5  6  07  06  05  04  03  02

# Table of Contents

# Learn about:

- **Monster truck uses**

- **Monster truck size**

- **Building a monster truck**

# CHAPTER 1

# Monster Trucks

Two monster trucks pull up to the starting line. Thousands of fans cheer as the drivers prepare for the race to begin. The drivers rev their engines as they wait for the green starting light. The sound of the engines roars throughout the stadium.

The light turns green. The drivers stomp down on the gas pedals. Dirt flies up from behind the trucks' huge tires. In a moment, the trucks go over a ramp. They sail over rows of junk cars. The trucks land on another ramp and race to the finish line.

Monster trucks are pickup trucks on giant wheels.

## About Monster Trucks

Monster trucks are pickup trucks with giant tires. Drivers race these trucks in events held around the United States and Canada. Drivers also show off monster trucks in special events such as car crushing. The trucks' giant wheels smash junk cars in these events.

An average monster truck is about 11 feet (3.4 meters) high and 12 feet (3.7 meters) wide. A standard pickup truck is about half this size. A monster truck weighs about 9,500 pounds (4,300 kilograms). A standard pickup truck weighs about 4,000 pounds (1,800 kilograms).

Monster trucks can reach speeds of about 75 miles (121 kilometers) per hour.

Their engines are about ten times more powerful than standard truck engines. Monster trucks can jump as high as 30 feet (9.1 meters) off ramps.

**Monster trucks can reach speeds of 75 miles (121 kilometers) per hour.**

**Monster trucks must be strong enough to safely land after high jumps.**

## Cost and Competition

Monster trucks are designed to be sturdy and powerful. They must be strong enough to safely land after high jumps. They also must be fast enough to win races.

Designers and engineers work together to design monster trucks. They may need more than a year to build one truck. The trucks can cost more than $100,000.

Most monster truck drivers compete in races. Some races take place on straight tracks. The fastest monster truck with the longest jump usually wins. Other race tracks have turns. Monster trucks tip over easily. Drivers must be careful to keep their trucks upright during turns.

Monster truck drivers also take part in freestyle and exhibition events. In these events, drivers show off the trucks' abilities. They may show how far a monster truck can jump. Car crushing events show how easily a monster truck can destroy a row of junk cars.

# Learn about:

- 4X4 trucks

- Bigfoot

- Changes to monster trucks

CHAPTER 2

# Early Models of Monster Trucks

The first monster truck was built in the 1970s. It was named Bigfoot. At first, Bigfoot's driver had no one to race. He just showed his giant truck to people around the world.

Soon, other people began building their own monster trucks. The drivers started holding races. Drivers and engineers kept improving the trucks. Today, monster trucks are a big business. Fans spend millions of dollars each year to attend monster truck events. Drivers can earn thousands of dollars in prize money for competing in races.

# Bigfoot

Bob Chandler built Bigfoot in the mid-1970s. He owned a business that repaired 4x4 trucks. These trucks have four-wheel drive. Their engines power all four wheels. Today, four-wheel drive trucks are common. But in the 1970s, few people owned 4x4 trucks.

Chandler wanted to interest people in his business and in 4x4 trucks. He put his 4x4 truck in front of his shop. He started adding equipment to the truck. He gave it big tractor tires and axles. Axles connect the wheels to the truck.

Chandler sometimes raced his 4x4. His friends called him "Bigfoot" because he pressed hard on the gas pedal during races. Chandler liked the name. He painted it on the side of his truck. He started calling the truck "Bigfoot."

Chandler continued to make improvements to Bigfoot. He added larger tires and a more powerful engine. Soon, it was too large to race against standard 4x4s. Instead, Chandler drove the truck around to show off his work. Bigfoot quickly became popular. People paid money just to see it.

Some people then built their own monster trucks. They based the trucks on Bigfoot. Chandler also built more monster trucks. He named each one Bigfoot. Today, he has more than 15 Bigfoots.

**Bigfoot was the first monster truck.**

**Car crushing was the first type of monster truck event.**

## Changes

Car crushing was the main monster truck event in the late 1970s and early 1980s. People built their trucks to be very heavy for this purpose. They used heavy metals such as steel. These trucks weighed as much as 18,000 pounds (8,165 kilograms).

Monster truck racing became popular in the mid-1980s. The heavy trucks were too slow for racing. People looked for ways to make the trucks lighter. They built new trucks of lightweight materials such as fiberglass. These lighter trucks were faster than the old trucks.

People also stopped using modified pickup trucks as monster trucks. They built trucks specially designed to be monster trucks. These trucks were larger and better suited for monster truck competitions.

Monster trucks' popularity grew throughout the 1980s. Monster truck events soon were common across North America. Fans attended monster truck events in large stadiums. They also watched the trucks on TV.

# Learn about:

- **Monster truck teams**

- **Monster truck bodies**

- **Supercharged engines**

# CHAPTER 3

# Designing a Monster Truck

Today, monster trucks are more carefully built than they were in the 1970s. Early monster truck designers just added parts to standard pickup trucks. Today, designers buy parts that are specially made for monster trucks.

People no longer build monster trucks alone. They hire teams of people to build and maintain the trucks. Engineers and designers create plans to build monster trucks. Engineers and mechanics then use these plans to build the trucks. They use custom parts. These parts are specially made by a company for the monster truck.

## Body Parts

The chassis is the most important part of a monster truck. The chassis is the truck's frame. It holds all of the other parts together. The chassis usually is made of a strong metal such as steel. A monster truck will fall apart if the chassis is not strong enough.

The body is the part that gives a monster truck its shape. The body covers the chassis. It covers the engine and helps protect the driver during accidents. Monster truck bodies once were made of metal. But today, designers use fiberglass. This material weighs less than metal. Artists paint colors and shapes on the body. The paint job makes each monster truck look different.

The large tires usually are the first thing people notice about a monster truck. Most monster truck tires are built for large farm machinery. Monster trucks have oversized wheels and axles to hold these tires.

The drivetrain provides engine power to the axles. Drivetrains of some vehicles power only two of the wheels. But monster trucks have drivetrains that power all four wheels.

A monster truck must have a strong suspension system. This system of springs and shock absorbers attaches the wheels to the chassis. It keeps the truck steady over rough ground. The suspension system also softens the landing after a truck takes a jump.

**A monster truck must have a strong suspension system.**

## The Engine

Most monster trucks have eight-cylinder
engines. A cylinder is a pipe-shaped chamber
where fuel is burned. Spark plugs cause fuel
inside each cylinder to explode. These small
explosions cause pistons inside the cylinder
to move up and down. This movement
creates power. The drivetrain delivers the
engine's power to the axles. The axles then
turn the wheels.

Monster truck engines are larger and
more powerful than standard truck engines.
Mechanics modify monster truck engines
to give them this additional power. They

may bore the cylinders. The mechanics grind down the inside walls of the cylinders to make them larger. A larger cylinder can create a larger explosion.

Most monster truck engines also have superchargers. These small devices blow extra air and gas into the cylinders. The extra air and gas cause larger explosions.

People measure an engine's power in horsepower. Monster truck engines with superchargers can produce as much as 1,600 horsepower. This amount is almost 10 times more than a standard truck can produce.

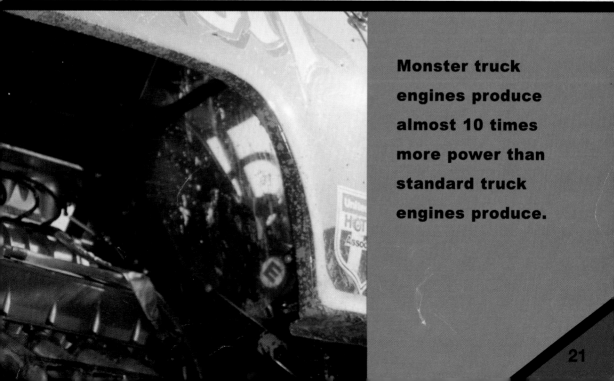

Monster truck engines produce almost 10 times more power than standard truck engines produce.

# Learn about:

- Car crushing

- Monster truck races

- Freestyle competition

# CHAPTER 4

# Monster Trucks
# in Competition

During the early 1980s, car crushing was the main monster truck event. At first, monster trucks crushed cars at events such as drag races and demolition derbies. The monster trucks were not the main event. But soon, fans wanted to see the monster trucks more than the main events. People began creating events just for monster trucks. They called them "monster truck wars." The wars were not official competitions. But monster truck drivers would compete to crush the most cars.

Car crushing no longer is common today. Monster trucks are lighter and faster than they once were. Now, monster trucks usually jump over rows of cars instead of crushing them.

**Monster trucks race on a variety of courses.**

## Monster Truck Races

Monster truck racing began in 1986. Trucks drove through obstacle courses as fast as they could. The courses included obstacles such as jumps and junk cars. Trucks did not race against each other. Each driver raced alone. Officials recorded each driver's time. The driver with the fastest time won.

Fans enjoyed watching the races. But they wanted to see monster trucks race against each other. Soon, two or more trucks raced at once. Each race was called a heat. The drivers raced against each other in heats until only two drivers remained. These drivers then raced against each other for the championship.

Monster truck courses differ from place to place.

Some are oval-shaped. Others are straight. Most monster truck courses have ramps and rows of junk cars. Drivers must study each course before they race. Studying helps them know exactly how to drive on each part of the course.

**Two monster trucks race side by side.**

## Freestyle

Freestyle events are the newest kind of monster truck competitions. During these events, drivers show off their trucks in a set amount of time. They do tricks such as jumps, wheelies, and donuts during this time. Drivers perform a donut by spinning around and around in a tight circle.

Freestyle competitions usually take place during larger monster truck events. They usually are not the main event. Officials sometimes select audience members to judge freestyle competitions. The audience members give drivers scores based on the tricks the drivers perform. This allows fans to take part in the events that they enjoy.

**Monster truck drivers show off their
trucks during freestyle competitions.**

# Pam Hutzell

In 1992, Pam Hutzell became the first female driver to race in a monster truck series. Her husband was racer Michael Vaters. Vaters raced a monster truck called Black Stallion. He built a second truck called Boogey Van. Hutzell told Vaters that she wanted to drive Boogey Van.

Hutzell qualified sixth in her first national event. She proved that she could race with men. In 1995, Hutzell finished fifth in her series. That year, she had a bad crash at a race in Detroit, Michigan. She ran Boogey Van into a wall. She was in the hospital for three days. But she returned to racing when she got out of the hospital. Hutzell still races today.

## Words to Know

**axle** (AK-suhl)—a rod in the center of a wheel around which the wheel turns

**chassis** (CHASS-ee)—the frame on which the body of a vehicle is built

**cylinder** (SIL-uhn-dur)—a hollow chamber inside an engine in which fuel burns to create power

**drivetrain** (DRIVE-trane)—the system of moving parts and belts that transfers power from the engine to the wheels

**fiberglass** (FYE-bur-glass)—a strong, lightweight material made of fine threads of glass

**heat** (HEET)—a race between two trucks

**modify** (MOD-uh-fye)—to change; people modify a vehicle or engine in order to make it faster or more powerful.

**suspension system** (suh-SPEN-shuhn SISS-tuhm)—the system of springs and shock absorbers that absorbs up-and-down movement from the axles

## To Learn More

**Koons, James.** *Monster Trucks.* Rollin'. Mankato, Minn.: Capstone Books, 1996.

**Mead, Sue.** *Monster Trucks and Tractors.* Race Car Legends. Philadelphia: Chelsea House, 1999.

**Savage, Jeff.** *Monster Trucks.* Action Events. Berkeley Heights, N.J.: Enslow Publishers, 2000.

## Useful Addresses

**Monster Truck Racing Association**
P.O. Box 2401
Florissant, MO  63032

**Performance Motorsports**
P.O. Box 713
Yorkton, SK  S3N 2W8
Canada

**SFX Motor Sports Group**
P.O. Box 6797
Aurora, IL  60598

## Internet Sites

**Bigfoot—The Original Monster Truck**
http://www.bigfoot4x4.com

**Monster Truck Racing Association**
http://www.truckworld.com/mtra

**Monstertrucks.net**
http://www.monstertrucks.net

## Index